Flip the Flaps
Jungle
Animals

Jinny Johnson and Nicki Palin

KINGFISHER

NEW YORK

KINGFISHER
LONDON & NEW YORK

Copyright © 2009 by Kingfisher
Published in the United States by Kingfisher,
175 Fifth Ave., New York, NY 10010
Kingfisher is an imprint of Macmillan Children's Books, London.

Consultant: David Burnie

First published in hardback in 2009 by Kingfisher
This edition published in 2012 by Kingfisher

Distributed in the U.S. and Canada by Macmillan, 175 Fifth Ave., New York, NY 10010

LIBRARY OF CONGRESS CATALOGING-IN-PUBLICATION DATA
Johnson, Jinny.
Flip the flaps jungle animals / written by Jinny Johnson ; illustrated
by Nicki Palin.
p. cm.
Includes index.
1. Jungle animals--Juvenile literature. I. Palin, Nicki, ill. II.
Title. III. Title: Jungle animals.
QL112.J54 2009
591.734--dc22
2009046931

ISBN 978-0-7534-6859-3

Kingfisher books are available for special promotions and premiums. For details contact:
Special Markets Department, Macmillan, 175 Fifth Avenue, New York, NY 10010.

For more information, please visit www.kingfisherbooks.com

Printed in China
3 5 7 9 8 6 4 2
2TR/1212/UNTD/LFA/128MA

Contents

Life in the jungle

Jungles are big forests that grow in places where it is very hot all the time. It rains almost every day, too, so jungles are always wet. In fact, another name for a jungle is "rainforest."

There are thousands of plants in a rainforest.

parrots

golden lion tamarins

sloth

giant anteater

4

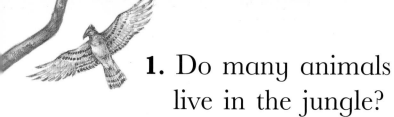

1. Do many animals live in the jungle?

2. Do some of them live in the trees?

emerald tree boa

3. What happens at night in the jungle?

The jungle at night

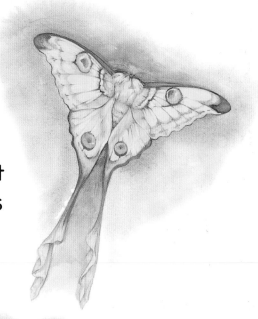

The comet moth flies at night.

The tarsier has big eyes for seeing in the dark.

The fishing bat snatches fish from the water.

Brilliant birds

Some of the world's most
amazing and colorful birds
live in jungles. But it can
be hard to spot them in the
tangled trees. Parrots, toucans,
hummingbirds, and birds of
paradise all live in the jungle.

**male bird
of paradise**

**female bird
of paradise**

6

harpy
eagle

1. Yes. More kinds of animals live in jungles than anywhere else on earth.

2. Yes. Many jungle animals live in the trees. Some of them never come down!

3. It's very dark—but busy! A lot of jungle creatures sleep during the day and wake up at night.

The jungle at night

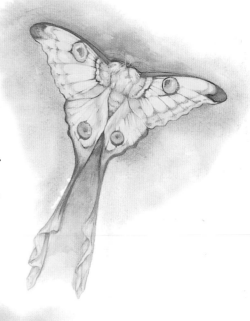

The comet moth flies at night.

The tarsier has big eyes for seeing in the dark.

The fishing bat snatches fish from the water.

5

Brilliant birds

Some of the world's most
amazing and colorful birds
live in jungles. But it can
be hard to spot them in the
tangled trees. Parrots, toucans,
hummingbirds, and birds of
paradise all live in the jungle.

**male bird
of paradise**

**female bird
of paradise**

6

hanging
upside down

1. Which are the most beautiful jungle birds?

2. Why do birds of paradise have colorful feathers?

3. What do jungle birds eat?

1. Male birds of paradise have some of the most spectacular feathers of all.

2. Males show off their colorful feathers to attract females. This one hangs upside down and rocks back and forth.

3. Many jungle birds get their food from plants. Their beaks are specially shaped to help them gather their food.

Beak shapes

hummingbird

sucking nectar with its long, thin beak

toucan

picking berries with its long beak

parrot

cracking a nut with its strong beak

7

Apes and monkeys

Apes and many kinds of monkeys live in jungles. Gorillas, chimpanzees, and orangutans are all apes. Fruit and leaves are their favorite foods. Apes are our closest relatives in the animal kingdom.

durian fruit

mother and baby orangutan

8

1. What is the difference between apes and monkeys?

2. How does an orangutan move around the jungle?

3. What do apes and monkeys do all day?

swinging
from a vine

1. Apes do not have tails, but most monkeys have long tails.

2. She swings from tree to tree using her long arms. Her arms are almost twice as long as her body!

3. Looking for food takes up most of the day, but they also play, groom each other, and rest.

Daytime activities

chimpanzee

using a stick to collect insects to eat

gorillas

taking a midday nap

squirrel monkey

grooming her baby

9

River life

A huge river flows through this jungle. It may look calm, but it is full of life, with huge snakes, crocodiles, and many fish. People can use rivers to travel through the jungle, too.

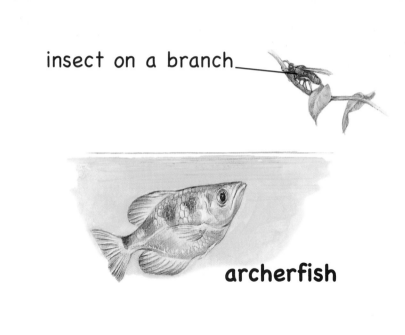

insect on a branch

archerfish

anaconda snake

capybaras

caiman hiding underwater

10

jet of water

caiman attacks

1. How does an archerfish catch its food?

2. Which are the fiercest animals in the river?

3. What other creatures live in jungle rivers?

1. The archerfish spits at an insect and knocks it down into the water. Then the fish gobbles up the insect.

2. Caimans are fierce animals. They lie with only their eyes and nose above the water, then make a surprise attack.

3. Many kinds of animals swim in jungle rivers, including piranhas.

Other animals in the river

Piranhas have sharp teeth.

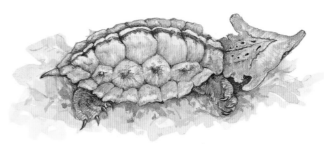

The matamata turtle looks like a clump of bark and leaves.

River dolphins eat fish, crabs, and turtles.

Jungle hunters

Many jungle creatures feed on leaves, flowers, and fruit. But there are plenty of meat eaters around, too. They hunt the plant-eating animals.

tiger

jaguar mom and cubs

12

1. Why do jungle cats have spots and stripes?

2. Which are the biggest hunters in the jungle?

3. What other hunters are there in the jungle?

tiger hiding in grass

jaguar roaring to scare
other animals away

1. Spots and stripes help big cats hide among jungle plants as they sneak up on their prey.

2. The tiger is the biggest jungle hunter of all. But jaguars are almost as large.

3. Birds hunt in the treetops, and ocelots hunt lower down. Bush dogs catch food on the forest floor.

spectacled owl

ocelot

bush dog

13

Insects
and spiders

There are more insects than any other type of animal in the jungle—and a lot of spiders, too. Ants, beetles, butterflies, and many others live on every tree as well as on the forest floor.

leafcutter ant

**The forest floor
is full of life.**

termites

beetle

bees

grasshopper

butterfly

1. What do leaf-cutter ants do with the leaves they collect?

2. Are there big spiders in the jungle?

3. How do insects hide from their enemies?

katydid

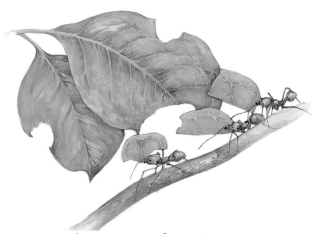

ants carrying leaves

butterfly
flying away

goliath
bird-eating
spider

1. They take them to their nest and chew them up. Then they grow fungi (tiny mushrooms) on the leaves for food.

grasshopper
hopping away

2. Yes. The largest spider in the world, the goliath bird-eating spider, is as big as a dinner plate!

3. Often they are disguised to look like something else, such as a flower.

katydid

Insects hiding

Can you find the flower mantis?

Can you see the stick insect?

15

Frogs, snakes, and lizards

These creatures like to live in warm, damp places, so jungles are just right. Many spend time up in the trees as well as on the ground. Snakes are good climbers—even though they have no legs.

flying lizard

green palm viper

1. Does a flying lizard really fly?

2. What do snakes eat?

green spiny lizard

3. Why are some frogs so brightly colored?

gliding through the air

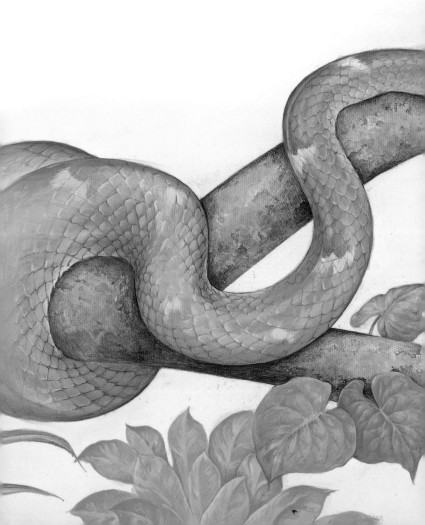

1. It doesn't really fly but can glide through the air from tree to tree. It uses flaps on its body like a parachute.

Tree frogs can be . . .

green and black

2. Snakes are meat eaters. They catch other animals and swallow them whole.

strawberry-red

blue

3. These frogs are very poisonous. Their bright colors warn other animals that they are not safe to eat!

yellow and black

17

Index